Are we running out of water?

Written by Isabel Thomas

Illustrated by El Primo Ramón

Foreword by Professor Sara Hughes, University of Michigan

EARTHAWARE
KIDS

A message from Professor Sara Hughes
Water and Climate Scientist, University of Michigan

Sara is a water scientist. She studies how we look after our water in a changing climate, especially in towns and cities. She works with other scientists and with world leaders to come up with ideas that will protect water supplies in the future.

Water is our planet's most precious resource—it keeps us healthy, it helps plants and animals grow, and it is used in nearly every area of our daily lives. Everywhere we look we see water—life cannot survive without it. But the amount of water on our planet is not unlimited.

Fresh water use by humans over the last few thousand years has changed where water is found on our planet and how much is available for all plants and animals. We now use so much water that our water supplies are threatened—we are using more than we can replace.

Taking care of water is a big task. Our demands for it are growing and the climate is changing. We use vast amounts of water for people, making food, and the environment, but we must stop using more than is necessary. We must protect it from harmful chemicals. And we must make sure that the way we store, transport, and clean water will make it safe, affordable, and available to everyone for years to come. We need to take action now to protect our water.

When you have read this book and learned about all the ways water is central to our lives, I hope you will talk to others about the importance of water and its protection. Each one of us can make a difference—and, together, we can help protect the future of our planet's water supply.

Contents

Mind mapping 4

How much water is on Earth?   6

Earth's water 8
The water cycle 10
Pure water 12

Why do we need fresh water?   14

Life on Earth 16
Using water 18
Surviving in dry places 20
Water and the human body 22

Why do we use so much water?   24

Water for food 26
Water at home 28
Hidden water use 30

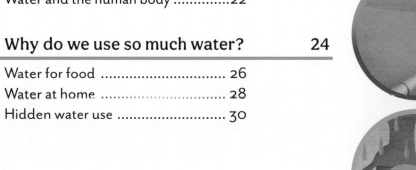

How do we get fresh water?   32

Finding water 34
Drilling for water 36
Water in our taps 38
Treating wastewater 40

Is there enough water?   42

Having enough water 44
Water quality 46
Using too much water 48
The effects of climate change 50
Water wars 52

Can we protect our water supply?   54

New technology 56
Saving water locally 58
Saving water around the world 60

What can I do to save water?   62

Be water smart 64
Use less of everything 66
Spread the word 68

Glossary 70
Index 72

Mind mapping

The reason this book is called Mind Mappers is because it is organized like a mind map. A mind map is a picture diagram that connects lots of different ideas. It is a very useful way to make complicated topics easy to understand. The mind map on this page looks at the question that is the title of this book—are we running out of water? It divides the subject into seven further questions, which are at the beginning of each chapter.

Follow the lines

Find the question that you would like to explore and follow the colored lines to look at the individual topics. For example, there are three main things people use water for—farming, in the home, and industry. Keep following the lines to see how these topics subdivide.

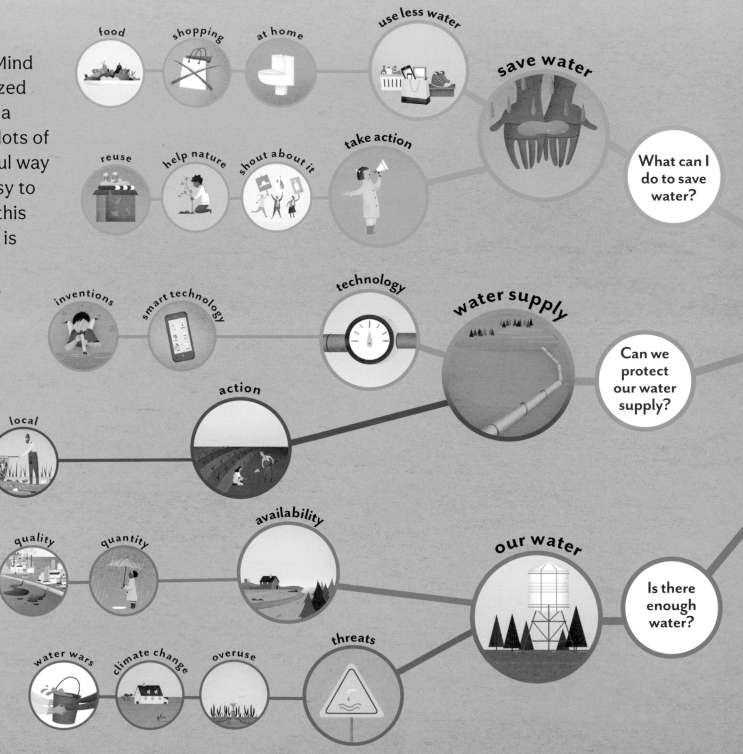

food · shopping · at home · use less water · save water · What can I do to save water?

reuse · help nature · shout about it · take action

inventions · smart technology · technology · water supply · Can we protect our water supply?

global · local · action

quality · quantity · availability · our water · Is there enough water?

water wars · climate change · overuse · threats

How much water is on Earth?

Earth's water

forms of water

solid

liquid

gas

water cycle

water movement

water content

The big picture
You can use this mind map to connect all the ideas in this book. It will help you to remember the main topics in the discussion about water.

our planet

life

plants

animals

water for life

survival

extreme living

human body

Why do we need fresh water?

Are we running **out of water?**

farming

crops

livestock

Why do we use so much water?

water use

in the home

everyday

leisure

How do we get fresh water?

industry

manufacturing

energy

fresh water

sources

drainage areas

underground water

water supply

clean water

dirty water

Connection circles
Throughout the book you will find colored connection circles leading you to different pages. These will help you join up the information, just like the mind map.

Go to page 10 to read about the water cycle.

water cycle

10

how much
water is on
Earth?

Water covers nearly three-quarters of our planet. So much sloshes around its surface that from space Earth looks blue. Water fills the oceans, forms ice caps, and scuds across the sky as clouds. Water is everywhere, but only a tiny bit is the fresh water needed by living things.

Earth's water

When you gaze across an ocean or dash through a shower of rain, Earth's water supply seems endless. But it is not always in a form that can be used by living things.

forms of water

Lots of things can be solid, liquid, or gas, but only water is found in all three forms at Earth's surface. This unusual property helps make life possible.

solid

liquid

gas

8

8

8

water cycle

Earth's water is always on the move in a process called the water cycle, which constantly recycles the planet's supply of fresh water.

water movement

water content

10

12

Earth's water

Water is everywhere. It rains from the sky and rushes in rivers. It floats as icebergs and plunges as waterfalls, drifts in steamy mists, and falls as snow. It crashes as waves, splashes as puddles, and clatters as hail. Water rises and falls with the tides and sparkles on the grass as dew. It is found inside the soil under our feet and the rocks that make our mountains. As it moves around, it shifts from solid to liquid to gas and back again when the temperature changes.

Inside water

If you could magnify a drop of water enough, you would see tiny molecules jostling about. Each is made of two hydrogen (H) atoms joined to an oxygen (O) atom. In a drop of water (H_2O), there are 1,500,000,000,000,000,000,000 (1.5 sextillion) water molecules!

H_2O

Solid

Just under two percent of Earth's water is solid ice. It is found in giant ice caps and ice sheets at the poles, and in glaciers and floating icebergs. It is also in the snow that permanently crowns the highest mountains.

Liquid

Most of Earth's water is a runny liquid. It fills ocean basins, flows under and over the land as rivers, and sits still in lakes, swamps, and soils.

The states of water

Water has no smell, no taste, and often no color. But it has special properties. It is the only substance found in three different forms, or states, at normal temperatures on Earth—as a solid, a liquid, or a gas.

Gas

When water is a gas, it exists as water vapor. Most of it is invisible to our eyes, but it can sometimes be seen as it forms mist and fog.

Water in the atmosphere

A very tiny fraction of Earth's water is found in the atmosphere. Most is no higher than 6 miles above sea level. An even smaller amount is even farther away from the surface at more than 25 miles up—that's about halfway to space!

water cycle

10

Moving and changing

As changing temperatures on Earth's surface heat and cool water, it can change state. It may go from ice to liquid water to vapor and back again. These changes mean water is always on the move.

There is water inside all living things.

Underground water

Water is not only found on the Earth's surface and in the air. Scientists have now found clues that there is water up to 600 miles beneath the ground.

Water connections

Earth is a blue planet. Water can be found almost everywhere on its surface, in the atmosphere, and deep underground. Water is always on the move in its different states.

The water cycle

Every day, Earth's surface is warmed by the Sun. And each night, the temperature falls again. This regular heating and cooling causes winds to blow, and drives an important process known as the water cycle. This constantly changes the state of water as it is recycled from the oceans, into the air, and back down again to land and sea.

Cooling down
As warm air rises, it quickly cools. This makes the water vapor it is carrying condense, or turn back into liquid water. Tiny droplets gather around specks of pollen or dust.

On the move
Water droplets bunch together, forming clouds. The water in the clouds is moved along by the wind.

Water's journey
A water molecule moving through the water cycle may spend a few weeks flowing in rivers, and 4,000 years in the ocean. But it only spends up to 11 days in the atmosphere before falling down to the ground.

Warming up
As it is warmed by the Sun, water evaporates, or changes to water vapor. It rises into the atmosphere.

Recycling water
The same water goes through the water cycle over and over again. The water you drink may have passed through a dinosaur, an Egyptian queen, a saber-toothed tiger—or all three!

Tyrannosaurus rex

Saber-toothed tiger

Egyptian queen Nefertiti

Mongol warrior Genghis Khan

35 →

water movement

Back to the surface

When the droplets grow to about the size of a pinhead, or become so cold they freeze, gravity takes over. Gravity is the force that keeps you on the ground and causes you to fall down and not up! The droplets or ice crystals fall to Earth's surface as rain, hail, or snow, and collect in lakes and rivers.

The water cycle was the same at the time of the dinosaurs as it is today.

Runoff

Water droplets trickle into streams and rivers, which flow downhill until they reach the oceans. They may also find their way into rocks, or become frozen as ice over land or sea.

Water connections

The water cycle is the journey that all water takes as it moves around our planet. In the process, water is constantly recycled as it evaporates, condenses, and returns to the ocean.

Scientist Albert Einstein

Artist Frida Kahlo

World leader Nelson Mandela

Climate activist Greta Thunberg

Pure water

Surprisingly, it is almost impossible to find pure water on Earth. A drop of water from a stream, lake, or ocean may look crystal clear, but zoom in and you will find all kinds of things mixed in it, from tiny bacteria to specks of dust. Most water also contains things it has come into contact with, such as salts. Seawater is too salty for us to drink, but we do not need fresh water to be completely pure for us to drink and use it.

10 water cycle

Inside a drop of water

A microscope reveals that a drop of seawater is home to thousands of tiny plants, algae, and bacteria. It is a miniature world full of life!

Why are the oceans salty?

Many substances dissolve in water as it flows over land, trickles through soil and rocks, and washes over the seabed. Salts dissolve in water especially easily. When water evaporates, any dissolved salts are left behind, which is why seawater has become salty over a long period of time.

Seawater

Most of Earth's water is in the oceans as salt water. All the seawater on the planet's surface is why Earth looks blue from space.

How things dissolve

Dissolving is a special kind of mixing. A substance breaks up into particles so tiny that it seems to disappear—like when you add sugar to a drink. Water is good at dissolving all kinds of substances.

The water cycle constantly filters Earth's supply of fresh water. It falls to the ground as rain or snow.

water at home

28

Fresh water

Lakes, rivers, snow, and ice are where fresh water is found. It contains far fewer dissolved salts than seawater. Just 2.5 percent of Earth's water is fresh water, but most of this is locked away in ice caps and glaciers, or found deep underground.

Water connections

Water has an amazing ability to dissolve things. This means that fresh water can easily become polluted. Fresh water from most sources must be filtered before we can drink it.

Drinking water

All plants and animals on land, including humans, need to drink fresh water. While Earth has plenty of water overall, fresh, clean water is a precious resource.

why do we
need fresh
water?

Plants and animals are made up of billions of cells, all working together. Every cell is mostly made of water. This water pushes outward, helping living things keep their shape. Water also lets cells share food and oxygen, remove waste, and control their temperature.

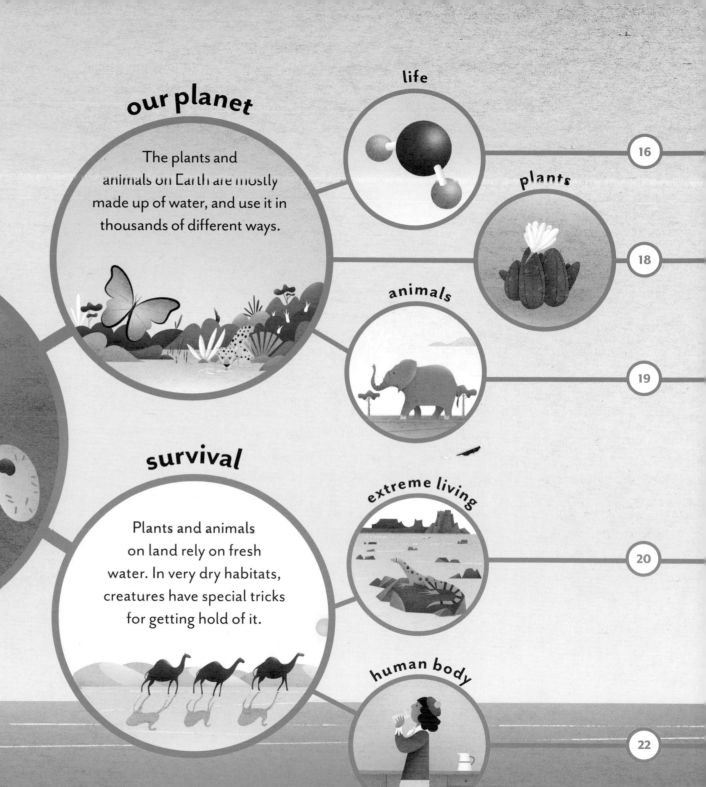

water for life

Wherever we find water on Earth, we also find life. All living things, including humans, need a source of water to grow and survive.

our planet

The plants and animals on Earth are mostly made up of water, and use it in thousands of different ways.

life

16

plants

18

animals

19

survival

Plants and animals on land rely on fresh water. In very dry habitats, creatures have special tricks for getting hold of it.

extreme living

20

human body

22

Life on Earth

Even from a million miles away, it is easy to spot differences between Earth and the other rocky planets of our solar system. Only Earth has blue oceans, flowing rivers, swirling clouds, and large, white ice caps. Only Earth has enough water on it to see from space. Water is why Earth is the only planet teeming with life. It is water that makes life on Earth possible.

Birds are 60% water

Many plants are 90% water

Living things

Despite your hard bones and strong muscles, you are at least two-thirds water. Water is a key building block of every living thing, which is why plants and animals must keep themselves topped up with water to stay alive. This is why living things are so thirsty!

Humans are 60–70% water

Some jellyfish are 95% water!

Fish are more than 70% water

topping up

22

Planet Earth

Life on Earth began in the oceans nearly 4 billion years ago. Today, millions of different plants and animals live on the land as well, but they still depend on water to survive.

Without water, Mercury cannot support life.

Mercury

Mercury has no liquid water, but an orbiting space probe has detected a little water ice at the bottom of its deepest craters.

Water connections

Earth is the only planet in our solar system that has life-giving water. Water is inside of and is used by all living things. Without water, life on Earth would not be possible.

using water

18

There may once have been life on Mars.

Venus

Venus once had a shallow ocean. The water evaporated and carbon dioxide collected in the atmosphere, heating the planet like a greenhouse.

Venus is too hot for liquid water, or for life.

Mars

Mars has polar ice caps like Earth. Its valleys and canyons tell us liquid water once flowed across the surface, too. This water escaped into space or was trapped in rocks a long time ago.

Using water

From lush vines to leopards, all living things need water to survive. Water is brilliant at dissolving substances such as oxygen and food so they can be transported in and out of cells and all around a living thing. Inside a cell, water plays an important part in the chemical reactions that give the plant or animal energy to perform tasks. There are many different ways in which plants and animals take in and use water.

Inside a plant cell

A plant cell is filled with cytoplasm, which is mostly water. It pushes on the insides of the cell, helping it keep its shape. A thin cell membrane holds in the liquid. A strong cell wall stops a cell from bursting like a water balloon.

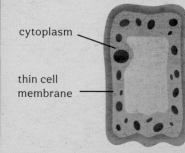

cytoplasm

strong cell wall

thin cell membrane

pure water

Making food

Green plants use the Sun's energy to split water molecules. They use part of the molecules to make food and the rest to send oxygen into the air.

Without water, a plant wilts.

12

Flowing upward

In a very narrow tube, water will flow upward, against the pull of gravity. This is called capillary action. It is how water travels from the roots of a plant to the leaves.

Roots take up water from the soil.

Water fills tiny gaps between soil particles.

Heat store

Water heats up and cools down slowly compared to most other substances. This helps living things to stay at a steady temperature.

life on Earth

Inside an animal cell

An animal cell is full of cytoplasm. It has only a thin cell membrane, but no strong cell wall. The animal's body carefully controls the amount of water in and around each cell.

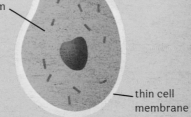

cytoplasm

thin cell membrane

Plant plumbing

Food made in leaves must be carried to every other part of a plant. In a tall tree, it may have to travel up 100 yards! Plants dissolve food in water to make a watery juice called sap. This then flows around the plant.

In and out

Animals take in water by drinking and eating. Blood and other body fluids are mainly water with different things mixed in. The fluids transport nutrients to each cell and carry waste away.

arowana fish

Under pressure

Air or water constantly squeeze living things. This pressure is greatest deep in the ocean. Water inside each cell balances the pressure, so things that live in water keep their shape.

Water connections

Water carries important substances in and out of the cells of living things. Inside the cells, water helps create the energy for the cells to do different tasks. Water does things that no other substance can.

Surviving in dry places

Deserts are the world's driest habitats. Every year, a typical desert gets ten times less rain than a typical rainforest. Most plants cannot survive with so little water, especially not big, thirsty plants such as trees. The lack of plants is what makes deserts look so deserted. But even the world's driest places, such as the Namib desert, are home to some plants and animals. These have special features or behaviors that help them collect water in surprising ways.

herd of oryx

Life in a cool desert

The Namib desert runs along Africa's Atlantic coast. Although it is cool, it is one of the world's driest places. Some years, no rain falls at all. Very few humans live in this rocky, sandy landscape, but some plants and animals have found ways to get the water they need.

Water from food

There is water in prey for desert creatures. The Namaqua chameleon changes color to blend in with the desert sands. This helps it stalk the worms, beetles, and locusts it eats.

Harvesting fog

In deserts along the coast, fog often blows across the land. A darkling beetle sticks its bottom in the air and waits. Dew condenses from the fog, becoming liquid on its bumpy wings, then trickles down toward its mouth.

water cycle

Saving water

Desert mammals waste as little water as possible. Golden moles make drier droppings and more concentrated urine than moles that do not live in deserts.

Extreme living

Many deserts are both hot and windy. Any water at the surface evaporates and is carried away faster than it is replaced by falling rain.

life on Earth

Water sources

Oryx can go for days without water. These antelopes get water from the plants they eat, and sometimes by digging for water underground.

Water connections

Desert plants and animals live life in delicate balance. Water is vital for their survival. Even a tiny change to their habitat can have a dramatic effect. If humans harm desert plants, desert insects and larger animals can lose their water source.

Storing water

The two thick leaves of a lithops plant store lots of water. These living stones have a pebbly appearance that helps hide them from thirsty animals.

Self-watering

A welwitschia plant grows just two long leaves that the wind splits into segments. Sea fog condenses on the leaves and trickles into the soil. There, the water is soaked up by the plant's sprawling roots.

Welwitschias can live for 2,000 years!

Temperature balance

Sengi, or elephant shrews, burrow into the sand to keep cool by day and warm by night. They get water by feeding on insects and other creepy-crawlies.

Water and the human body

Like other living things, humans are mainly made of water. It is found inside your cells and surrounding all your organs and tissues. It is also the main ingredient in blood, which carries the essential minerals and nutrients you need to all parts of your body. You need to take in up to two quarts of water every day to keep up your water reserves and stay healthy. A human can only survive for around three days without drinking water.

Tears
Tears do important work. As well as showing how you feel, they keep your eyes clean by washing out dirt and chemicals.

Topping up
Your body loses water as it makes urine and sweat. You also lose water vapor every time you breathe out. If you feel thirsty, you are already dehydrated and you need to replace the water by taking a drink.

getting water

38

Smoothing the way
The saliva, or spit, in your mouth and the slippery mucus that coats passages in your body are mostly water. They help food move through your digestive system. Other fluids help your joints move and cushion your brain and eyes against shocks.

Keeping cool
Water plays an important role in controlling body temperature. The water in your blood and tissues carries heat away from your muscles. Your skin releases sweat, which cools your blood as it evaporates.

If you are playing sports, you may lose a small cupful of water from your lungs every hour.

Transport system
Water makes your blood runny. This means it can be pumped quickly around your body to deliver food and oxygen, and collect waste.

Your watery body
Some parts of your body contain more water than others. Even your teeth are 8–10 percent water!

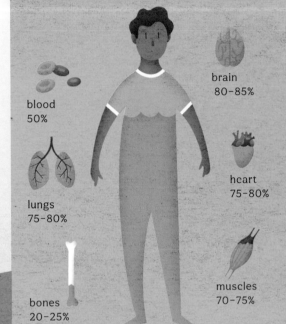

blood 50%

brain 80–85%

heart 75–80%

lungs 75–80%

muscles 70–75%

bones 20–25%

drinking water

45

Water connections
Every human needs to take in fresh water each day to replace the water their body uses and loses. It is vital to replace the water by drinking or eating. A third of the water you take in will usually come from food.

why do we use so much **water?**

Every day we use water for drinking, washing, cooking, and cleaning—but our water needs do not stop there. Water helps make everything we buy or use. That includes electricity and clothing, food and the internet, paper, and transport.

farming

Farming crops and animals for food, clothing, and other things is the thirstiest activity of all.

crops

livestock

water use

The amount of water people use depends on what they are using the water for. Everything we produce, eat, buy, and make uses water in some way.

in the home

At home we use water for drinking, cooking, heating, and flushing toilets. Hobbies need water too.

everyday

leisure

industry

Producing energy, digging for raw materials, and making things in factories all use water. Even the internet relies on water!

manufacturing

energy

Water for food

We use more water for farming than for anything else. In fact, almost three-quarters of all our fresh water is used for watering crops—or irrigation—and looking after livestock. As world population increases, we will need even more food. By 2050, farms may need to produce double the food they do now. At the same time, a lack of water in some places threatens to leave people without enough to eat. The race is on to find less thirsty ways to farm both crops and animals.

Central heating for crops
Not all water used for farming is sprayed onto crops. Water is also used to heat greenhouses and cool the huge buildings where crops are stored.

Crops are planted at times when rainfall is highest.

Growing crops

Farmers need water to make their crops grow. In some areas, enough water comes from rainfall. In drier places, farmers may have to take water from rivers for irrigation. This provides the extra water to help produce healthy crops.

Crop spraying
Many crops are sprayed with pesticides, which are chemicals dissolved in water. This is a major cause of water pollution because the chemicals run into rivers.

irrigation

51

Raising livestock

Producing animal products, such as meat, dairy, and eggs, uses about one and a half times more water than is needed to produce plant-based foods. Animals need water all year round to drink. Farmers also have to wash and clean the buildings the animals are kept in, as well as water crops to feed them.

Processing food

Water use does not end at the farm gates. Farms and food producers use water to wash crops to sell, process meat in factories, and make food packaging.

Red meat

It takes 4,000 gallons of water to make just eight beef burgers. That's twenty times more water than it takes to grow the same amount of cereals or root vegetables.

eat less meat

Dairy

In a dairy, fresh water is used for cooling and cleaning. It takes around 8 quarts of water to produce just 1 quart of milk.

Water connections

As the world's number-one water guzzler, farming is at high risk of running out of water. It is important to make farming less water-intensive, and to avoid the pollution of water supplies.

66

Water at home

An average person uses dozens of gallons of water every day. Some people use much less, and some much, much more. We drink water and use it to wash, cook, clean, heat, or cool our surroundings, and flush toilets. We also use it to water plants and fill pools so that we can enjoy it in our leisure time. Water plays a big part in almost everything we do at home.

Drinking

In many countries, water is cleaned before it reaches the taps, making it safe to drink.

In the kitchen

Water is often used in cooking, but the biggest waste is in washing up. Some kitchen taps can shoot out up to 6 gallons of water every minute!

Cleaning

From dishwashers to mops and sprays, we use lots of water in our quest to clean up after ourselves.

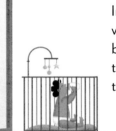

keeping cool

23

Sport and play

A lot of water is used for fun. But when it is dry and there is not much rain, cutting down on water use that is not essential for our needs is a great way to save water.

Many gardens have plants that do not grow there naturally, and that cannot survive on rainwater alone.

What is a water footprint?

The amount of water each of uses in our daily lives is called our water footprint. Pets have a water footprint, too. Most of this water is used to produce pet food.

delivering water

39

Heating and cooling

Central heating and air conditioning systems use a lot of water. They may be responsible for up to a quarter of the water used in a building.

In the bathroom

More than a third of water in our homes is used for bathing and showering. Another third is used to flush the toilet.

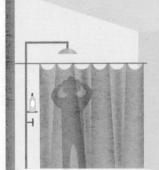

Washing

The water footprint of our clothes goes up every time we wash them. Almost a fifth of the water we use sloshes around in the machine before going down the drain.

Water connections

Water is essential in our daily lives and we need it to keep healthy. But if we want to reduce our water footprint, cutting water use at home is a good place to start.

Hidden water use

A huge amount of water is needed to make the things we use every day in our homes, from clothes and toys to electricity and the internet. It takes more than a gallon of water just to produce one plastic bottle–far more water than the bottle can hold. Water is used by farms, factories, and other industries that are often far away from our homes, sometimes even in different countries. In parts of the world with lots of rainfall, such as Europe, industry uses almost as much water as farming. Making and transporting the things they produce forms part of our water footprint.

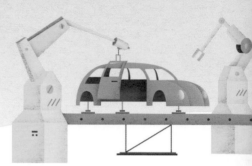

Cars

It takes nearly 50,000 gallons of water to produce just one car. More than 78 million cars are made around the world each year.

About a fifth of the world's fresh water is used to make things we use in our everyday lives.

28 water at home

Mining and quarrying

When we dig raw materials out of the ground, water is used in many different ways. It helps wash a "slurry" of mined rock out of the earth, and can be used for building materials for our homes.

Staying online

Video calls, streaming, and gaming online rely on huge buildings filled with computers. Millions of gallons of water are used every day to keep these places cool.

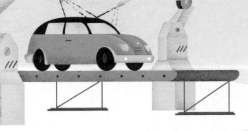

It takes around 600 gallons of water to make a single car tire.

Biofuels are made from thirsty crops such as sugar cane.

Generating power

All kinds of energy production rely on fresh water. It cools steam in power stations and is used to extract and process fuels. This includes green sources of energy, including the manufacture of hydrogen fuel, or to water biofuel crops.

use less energy

67

Paper

One sheet of paper may take more than 2 gallons of water to produce. The fast-growing trees used to make it drink water from the soil. In paper mills, water is used for pulping and bleaching.

Clothes

The textiles industry makes clothes and other things out of fabric. It is one of world's biggest water users. Cotton is a particularly thirsty crop, and the process of making a cotton T-shirt or a pair of jeans uses huge amounts of water.

Water connections

Industry is a major water guzzler. The water it uses often does not have to be as clean or fresh as the water used by farms and in homes. This makes it an important area for saving water.

how do we
get fresh
water?

There are 8 billion of us in the world, and we all need clean, fresh water! Our water comes from lots of different places, including streams, reservoirs, and wells. For many of us, water is cleaned and treated before gushing out of the taps in our homes.

fresh water

Many people around
the world take their fresh water
from rivers, lakes, springs, and wells.
For others, it is carried through
pipes or containers to their homes.

sources

Rivers, reservoirs,
lakes, and underground
water are important sources of
fresh water, topped up by rain.

drainage areas

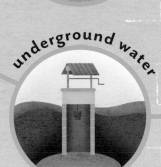

underground water

water supply

Water industries
are responsible for cleaning
fresh water before it reaches our
taps. They also take away the dirty
wastewater that leaves our homes.

clean water

dirty water

Finding water

No matter where we live, we are all in a watershed. A watershed is an area of land that drains all the water from rain or snow to a certain place. This place can be a lake, river, or ocean, or even into the ground. Our source of water depends on the watershed we live in. Fresh water might be taken from lakes, streams, or melting glaciers. It might be groundwater pumped out using a well, or water from human-made stores such as reservoirs.

water cycle

10

Water sources

In the past, people had to settle near a freshwater source, or travel from place to place to find water. Now most people have it piped straight to their homes, sometimes from many miles away.

Groundwater

If water finds its way into the spaces in soils and rocks, most of the water in a watershed might be found underground. Some of this groundwater will return to the surface through springs and rivers.

Storing water

Reservoirs are large lakes that store water until it is needed, and are usually built by people. Dams control the flow of water from rivers into reservoirs.

delivering water

39

Water flows down

The downward force of gravity causes water to flow from higher areas of land toward low-level bodies of water. Hills or mountains divide the flow of water into different watersheds.

Water quantity

The amount of fresh water available lower in a watershed depends on how much rain or snow has fallen higher up. The quantity removed by evaporation or by people as it flows down also affects availability.

Water quality

The cleanliness of local water sources depends on what is happening higher up in that watershed. Homes, farms, industries, and mines may pollute the water, which is then carried downstream. It is important that watersheds are carefully managed to keep them healthy.

Water connections

To understand water supply, we need to understand watersheds. Human activities can have a big impact on the quality and quantity of water available in the low-level areas of a watershed.

Drilling for water

Almost all of the world's fresh liquid water is found underground, trapped in tiny spaces in soils and rocks. It is harder to access than surface water in rivers and lakes, but we can get hold of it by digging a well or borehole into an aquifer. This is a place where underground water moves easily through the rock. At least half of the world's population depend on aquifers to supply them with clean, fresh water.

everyday water use

30

Water table

The level below the surface where water can be found is called the water table. It changes with the seasons, weather, and climate.

Rocks and soils

The type of rocks below the ground have a huge impact on how easy it is to get hold of groundwater. Some rocks contain cracks that water can pass through, which allows it to collect and form an aquifer.

Aquifer

A good, reliable source of groundwater is called an aquifer. Wells only work if they are dug into aquifers. The water rises up naturally if it is tightly contained by the rocks around it. Pumps are sometimes used to help bring water to the surface.

drained water
40

Shaping history

In the past, towns and cities sprang up near sources of surface water such as rivers and lakes. Today, many large communities rely on hidden aquifers. These underground stores need to be carefully managed to make sure water is not taken out too quickly, so they have time to refill.

Hot surfaces

Modern cities and towns have large paved areas, such as roads, sidewalks, and parking lots. Rainwater may evaporate or run off into rivers before it can seep underground to refill aquifers.

Natural springs

In some places, water from an aquifer is pushed to the surface as a spring. People can easily get hold of the water, but the aquifer is more easily polluted.

Danger of collapse

When too much water is taken from an aquifer, the soil or rock may collapse into the empty spaces left behind. This can cause the surface directly above the aquifer to subside, or sink.

A full aquifer supports the land above it.

If an aquifer is empty, the land above may sink.

Water connections

Aquifers are important sources of fresh water, especially for towns and cities. They need to be carefully managed to make sure that water is not taken more quickly than it is replaced by rain seeping underground.

28

water at home

Water in our taps

For many people, a clean water supply is provided by large companies or governments. Fresh water drawn from natural or human-made sources is filtered and treated with chemicals to get rid of harmful bacteria. It is then delivered to people's homes and workplaces by a system of pumps and pipes. In these places, it is so easy to get water by turning on a tap that we rarely think about the people and organizations that are involved in getting it there.

A human right
The United Nations has declared that every human has a right to water. Nations are responsible for making sure that every person has safe, clean, and affordable water to drink and to keep healthy.

Water management
In many countries, clean water is managed and provided by the government. In other countries, businesses can bid to deliver water and other cleansing services to the people living in a certain area.

Cleaning the water
Before water can be piped to where it is needed, it must be cleaned. This is so that we do not get sick from water that contains harmful substances.

Caring for the environment
All water services need to think about how they avoid damage to the environment. Taking too much water from any source can cause serious harm to local animals and plants.

Who pays for our water?
In many places, home and business owners pay bills and taxes to fund water supply and drainage. Wealthy countries may also donate money to support regions that cannot raise enough to pay for their own water services.

desalination

57

Processing sea water
In some very dry parts of the world, salt is removed from sea water to turn it into fresh water. This desalination process is expensive because it uses huge amounts of energy.

Collecting water
Water services collect water from sources on the surface and below ground. Because the amount of rainfall varies from season to season, they may also dam rivers or build reservoirs. This is to make sure there is enough water available all year round.

Water connections
Access to water for drinking and cleanliness is a human right. Most people pay for clean, safe water to be supplied by water services. The water must be cleaned before it is piped to our taps for us to use.

Delivering water
Water services have to look after huge networks of pipes and pumps that are used to transport water to homes and other buildings. Leaks are a major problem, so frequent upkeep is needed.

Treating wastewater

The work of water services does not stop when fresh water reaches our taps. They are also responsible for dealing with all the wastewater that we drain or flush away. In many places, this dirty water is collected and sent to water treatment plants through underground drains, or sewers. Once the water has been cleaned to remove dirt and germs, it can be released into rivers, lakes, or seas to rejoin the water cycle. Some water is cleaned again and recycled straight back into the water supply.

What is in wastewater?

Wastewater is polluted. It may contain food scraps, plastic fibers, chemicals, medicines, and paints, as well as everything we flush down the toilet, or that is washed down road drains. Sometimes solid waste clumps together to form large "fatbergs" that can block the drains.

hidden water use

30

Cleaning process

Most treated wastewater is not clean enough to drink, but it should be clean enough to avoid harming the environment it is returned to. Sadly, this does not always happen.

At the water treatment plant

After filtering to remove large floating items, water goes through at least three different stages of treatment. These remove solid waste, any dangerous chemicals, and invisible bacteria.

Solids—mainly human waste—settle in large tanks.

Inside the tanks, friendly microbes feed on dangerous bacteria and pollutants, breaking them down.

polluted water

46 →

Wastewater's journey

After rushing down drains, wastewater flows through pipes and into large sewers. There, it mixes with our neighbors' wastewater before flowing to a water treatment plant.

The friendly microbes are removed from the water. Then the cleaned water is recycled or returned to nature.

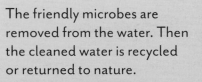

Water connections

Removing and cleaning wastewater is vital work carried out by water services. Yet a huge amount of the world's wastewater is dumped or overflows untreated into rivers, lakes, and oceans. It is a major source of water pollution.

is there
enough
water?

Although there is as much water on Earth as there has ever been, it is not evenly spread around the planet. Millions of people live in parts of the world where fresh water is scarce. Millions more do not have any access to clean, fresh water.

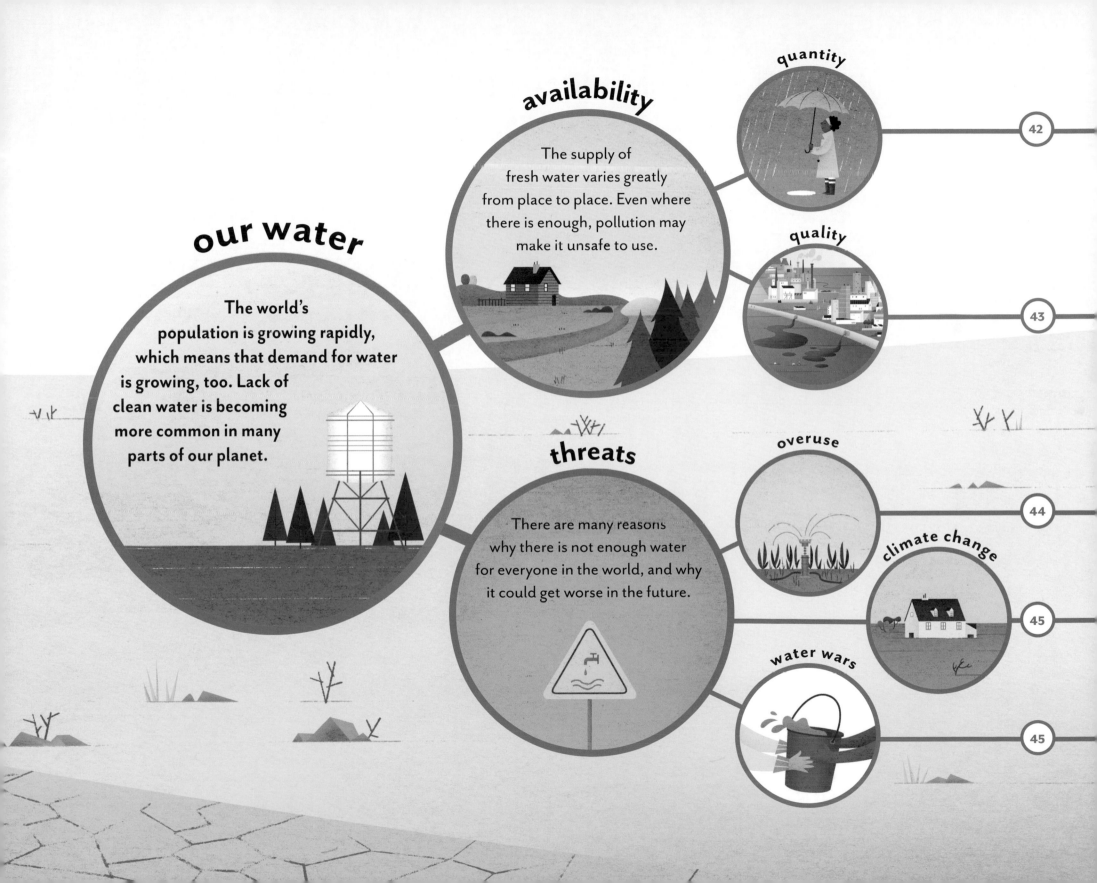

our water

The world's population is growing rapidly, which means that demand for water is growing, too. Lack of clean water is becoming more common in many parts of our planet.

availability

The supply of fresh water varies greatly from place to place. Even where there is enough, pollution may make it unsafe to use.

quantity

42

quality

43

threats

There are many reasons why there is not enough water for everyone in the world, and why it could get worse in the future.

overuse

44

climate change

45

water wars

45

Having enough water

Earth is a very watery place, but the fresh water we need is not spread out evenly. The water cycle delivers far more rain to some parts of the world than others, and it is difficult to transport this water long distances so everyone has enough. So while some people have plenty of water for washing, flushing the toilet, and drinking, millions of other people struggle to find enough water to drink.

finding water

34

Location lottery
Some people live in areas where more rain falls than they know what to do with. Attitudes to water vary hugely depending on where a person lives, and what kinds of activities they do.

Life with water
When clean, safe water is piped to our homes, we might take it for granted. We use it in almost every part of our lives, and often let some go to waste. But not everyone has the amount of water they really need.

Many gallons are used when people wash in showers and baths.

Gallons are wasted by leaving a tap running as we wash dishes.

Gallons of fresh, clean water are used to wash waste down toilets.

Water and hygiene

Pandemics such as COVID-19 remind us that washing our hands can save lives. But nearly 3 billion people around the world have nowhere to safely wash their hands, even in their homes.

collecting water
52

Water scarcity

Around half the world's population live in areas that are so dry they face severe water scarcity for at least one month every year. Water scarcity means that there is not enough water to meet demand.

Life without a water supply

In some places, lakes and reservoirs are left dry and cracked from overuse or lack of rain. For one in ten people, the nearest source of clean, affordable water is more than half an hour's walk away. A quarter of people around the world do not have a place to go to the toilet or wash in their homes.

Water connections

People need a reliable water supply for their everyday needs. But water is unevenly distributed around our planet. We need to work out how we can provide enough water to places that do not always have a steady supply.

Clothes are washed far more often than they need to be in water-hungry machines.

Tap water is used to give house plants a drink. They actually prefer rainwater.

Only a relatively small quantity of drinking water is used for drinking.

Water quality

People need water to be more than just fresh—it needs to be clean and free from dangerous pollution, too. Yet at least a quarter of people around the world drink polluted water every day because they have no choice.

Farm pollution

Every time it rains, animal waste and fertilizers are washed off farmland, often into rivers and lakes. These substances can destroy wildlife and natural habitats.

What is polluting our water?

The water we use can be polluted by chemicals, harmful microbes, or objects such as plastic waste. All three types of pollutants are usually added by humans, either by mistake or on purpose.

People pollution

We often use chemicals such as insect repellents and sunscreen in our daily lives. These find their way from our bodies into water when we swim or wash.

water at home

28

Sewage pollution

Human sewage is one of the main sources of water pollution. A third of all rivers are contaminated by germs from untreated sewage.

Drinking water danger

At least 122 million people take their drinking water directly from rivers and lakes. If that water is contaminated with sewage, it spreads diseases such as cholera, dysentery, and typhoid.

40

wastewater

How harmful is polluted water?

Every year, about 1 billion people become sick from drinking or using unsafe water, and almost 2 million die.

Industrial pollution

Factories, power stations, and mines use lots of water. When the water flows back into nature, it contains dangerous chemicals and sewage that harm wildlife and humans.

Wastewater

About 80 percent of wastewater around the world flows into rivers and oceans without being cleaned first. This includes chemicals and dirt washed off roads.

Fuel pollution

Oil and chemical spills pollute the water, and can be a disaster for birds and marine creatures such as fish, dolphins, and turtles. They may even destroy whole ecosystems, including coral reefs.

Plastic pollution

The litter we throw out can also pollute water, and contains huge amounts of plastic that takes hundreds of years to break down.

Water connections

People can be seriously harmed by diseases caused by polluted water. It is vital that we understand what causes water pollution so that we can take steps to prevent it.

aquifers

Using too much water

When more than a quarter of the fresh water in an area is being used by people, the area is said to be suffering from water stress. Sometimes water is used faster than the water cycle can replenish it. When that happens, water stress can lead to water scarcity, which is when there is not enough water to meet demand. The demand for fresh water in the world today is six times greater than it was 100 years ago, so both water stress and water scarcity are increasing.

Water on the move

Food is often transported around the world and eaten far from where it is farmed. This means the water locked inside crops and animal products is returned to the water cycle in a completely different place. Meanwhile, the farms the food came from suffer from a lack of water.

Dangers of overuse

Almost a third of the world's aquifers are being drained faster than local water cycles can top them up. Old, leaky pipework can make water losses even worse.

Destroying habitats

Many human activities threaten water supplies. Cutting down trees in forests in one part of the world can disrupt complex natural cycles that move air and water around the planet.

drought

51

Population growth
Demand for water is rising as the world's population grows. More than half of us live in areas where the water supply may not be able to meet demand in the future.

More money, more water
Over the last 100 years, water use has grown more than twice as fast as new babies are born. This is because billions more people can now afford to buy more water-hungry items, and have clean, fresh water at home.

Water in towns
Demand for water is high in towns and cities. In some of these places, there are freshwater sources but no systems to get the water to people. Wealthier people can afford to pay for water for themselves, but less well-off people still struggle to find enough.

Weather events
We often use more water at hotter times of year, but sometimes the rainy season may not arrive to refill water sources. Droughts can last for many years, meaning people cannot grow food for themselves, their cattle, or their sheep.

Water connections
Overuse of water and decreasing supplies are a growing problem that affects every continent. Even parts of the world with large freshwater sources are at risk.

water cycle

The effects of climate change

People burn vast amounts of coal, oil, and gas to power vehicles, factories, and homes. Burning these fossil fuels releases gases into the atmosphere, and these are causing temperature rises and changes in the climate worldwide. These changes have led to more extreme weather, including bigger storms, as well as melting glaciers and rising sea levels. Climate change is altering the distribution of water around the world, as events such as floods and droughts create water shortages in many more places.

Flooding

In recent years, climate change has caused heavier rainstorms, rising sea levels, and melting glaciers. These have all increased the risk of more destructive flooding in certain parts of the world.

The danger of floodwater

Flooding is when there is a sudden increase in surface water. It might seem strange that this can lead to water shortages, but floodwater washes pollutants into surface and groundwater, making them unsafe to use.

Water movement

Climate change is altering the movement of wind and water around Earth's surface. It is causing water to end up in places it is not normally found, which is what happens in floods.

Drought

A longer-than-usual period of low rainfall leading to a shortage of water is called a drought. Climate change is making droughts more frequent.

living in dry places

Dangers of drought

Higher temperatures are increasing the demand for water in many places. It is needed to drink and keep cool, but especially for irrigating crops.

What if we do nothing?

Drought caused by climate change is threatening our crops and food supplies because of a lack of water. Scientists have worked out that if we do not fight climate change, more than half the world's people will also be at risk from water stress by 2050.

Less surface water

During periods of drought, farmers struggle to get enough water to their fields and plants. Surface water sources such as lakes, reservoirs, and wetlands quickly dry up.

Water connections

Climate change is making water supply less certain. The effects can be seen in places already suffering water stress. Unless action is taken, water stress will become more widespread.

Water wars

Supplying everyone with enough clean, fresh water is one of the biggest problems facing the world. As governments, farms, industries, and individuals race to protect their water supplies, it is likely they will come into conflict with each other. The first water war happened more than 4,500 years ago when a city in Iraq changed the flow of a river to fill its canals, stopping water reaching another city in the process. Today's leaders face the same challenge—how to deal with water stress and scarcity without affecting other people's supply.

Water migration

When people face water-supply problems, many will choose to move nearer a reliable and clean source of water. Scientists think that by 2030 hundreds of millions of people will be at risk of having to move because of drought.

a human right

38

Ninety percent of countries in the world share water sources with at least one or two other countries.

Working together

To avoid fighting over water, communities and countries need to work together to look after shared water resources. This includes taking action to tackle climate change.

Storing water

Large dams are built across rivers to hold huge amounts of water and control when and where it flows. But sometimes the people building the dams do not consider how this will affect the water supplies of people living downstream.

Changing the water supply

Dams create a reliable water source for farmland and people upstream, but can reduce the amount of water reaching places downstream. This can lead to conflict.

Water trek

People who have been cut off from their usual water source often have to travel very long distances to find water.

Water connections

The world's water does not stick to the boundaries created by humans, and needs to be a shared resource. Countries will always need to work together to manage water sources and avoid water wars.

can we protect our water supply?

Problems with finding enough fresh water already affect large areas of the world. In the future, this problem will continue to grow unless we act now. There are many different ideas about how we can protect the world's water supply, which can be achieved by us all working together.

water supply

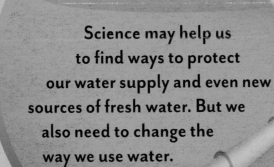

Science may help us to find ways to protect our water supply and even new sources of fresh water. But we also need to change the way we use water.

technology

Clever ideas can help us to look after our water supplies. It is vital that we find new methods of doing things to preserve our ecosystems.

smart technology

56

inventions

57

action

Decisions made in one place can affect people who live thousands of miles away. We must work together to protect our water supply.

local

58

global

60

New technology

For thousands of years, people have used new technology to help secure their supply of fresh water. The ancient Sumerians invented irrigation systems to water crops. The ancient Egyptians created chemical filters to purify water from the River Nile. The ancient Romans built aqueducts to carry water through hills and across valleys. Today's scientists and engineers are working just as hard to develop new answers to the problems of water stress and scarcity.

water quality

46

Saving water at home
Technology can help us to save water at home. Some ideas are very simple, such as fitting a water-saving gadget inside a toilet. Others are hi-tech, such as smart meters.

Smart meters monitor how much water is used and help us avoid waste.

Finding new water sources
Technology is helping us to find hidden sources of water. Scientists recently discovered a huge freshwater aquifer under the Atlantic Ocean, near the East Coast of the USA.

Saving water as a community
You've probably seen people withdraw cash from machines, but have you ever seen water withdrawn from one? Drinkwell Water uses smart technology to let people withdraw water from their machines. This helps reduce water loss in places where many people share a single water supply.

Improving water quality
LifeStraw® is a strawlike invention that filters water on the spot. It removes parasites to make water safe to drink.

Cloud seeding

The clusters of tiny droplets of fresh water that make up clouds do not always rain down where they are most needed. Cloud seeding changes this by adding substances to clouds to make raindrops form.

Saving water on farms

Smart irrigation technology uses satellites to monitor climate and rainfall from space. The information is sent to farmers' phones to help them use water only where and when it is needed.

Moving water

Some ideas are more ambitious. One is to tow giant icebergs to cities that are short of water. Icebergs have been nudged off course by ships before, but towing big ones long distances—and stopping them melting—will be much harder.

New types of crops

Farmers are working on using drought-resistant crops that need less water to grow. They may even grow plants without soil!

One desalination project uses wave-powered buoys at sea to produce fresh water.

Water from the sea

Seawater can be turned into fresh water by removing the salt. This is called desalination, and it uses lots of energy. If this energy comes from renewable sources, then desalination may become an important source of water in the future.

salt water

Water connections

There is no single science or technology that can solve the problems of water stress and scarcity. To protect the world's fresh water supply, we need to change the way we manage and use water, too.

Saving water locally

The best way to protect our local water supply is simple. We need to better manage the water that is already easy to reach and make it available to everyone. If we clean the water we have and waste less of it, we might not need so much overall. The international World Bank worked out that doing this would cost just one-thousandth of the world's total wealth. The benefits for everyone are more than equal the cost.

Looking after resources

We can all help to reduce water waste by fixing leaks in our homes. A single dripping tap can leak more than 1,000 gallons of water in a year, and a leaky toilet tank can waste 100 gallons of water a day!

leaky pipes

48

Using less water

It is possible to reduce local water use on a huge scale. Some places have shown that if they put careful plans in place to protect water supplies, they can cut the amount of water people use in half.

Reducing waste

In many countries, one-third to two-thirds of water leaks out of pipes before it reaches homes. This is an easy place to start saving water.

Cleaning up pollution

It is important to manage wastewater and stop pollution entering our water systems. Some cities have reduced pollution so much that people can swim in places that normally have dirty water, like harbors.

red meat

Planning new towns

Thinking about water is vital when building new homes and towns. Many town planners are beginning to realize how important it is to leave natural protections such as floodplains in place, rather than draining the land to build on it. Floodplains filter and store water, and protect the surrounding areas from floods.

Water connections

The ways we protect our local water supply start with thinking more carefully about how we use and manage water. Caring for nature is not just a nice thing to do—it is vital to help protect our water supply.

Protecting the habitats of dam-building beavers can help preserve water by stopping flooding.

Food choices

People in wealthier countries eat plenty of red meat. Farming the animals the meat comes from uses lots of fresh water. If we ate a little less red meat, this small change would make a big difference.

Saving water around the world

Our water supply usually comes from local sources, which are managed by local governments and water companies in one small area. But we know that water ignores human borders and boundaries. To protect the planet's water supply, people across the world need to work together. There are many water heroes already helping with efforts to save water and make sure there is a clean supply for everyone.

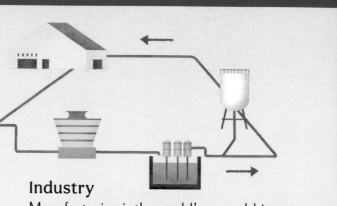

Industry
Manufacturing is the world's second-biggest user of water. Changes in industry, such as reusing water in factories, can show it is possible to save huge amounts of water.

Water heroes
All sorts of people in different jobs work hard to protect our water. They share smart ideas, take on new challenges, and help everyone to be aware of the importance of saving water.

plants for water-smart towns

drip irrigation

charity worker

industrialist

scientist

Environment groups
Some environmental groups help look after outdoor spaces. They restore wetlands, and encourage town planners to use plants that need less water and farmers to use better irrigation techniques.

Charities
People working for charities make sure everyone has access to clean water. They raise money for important new projects such as solar-powered water pumps, and try to convince governments to make new laws about water.

solar-powered water pump

spread the word

68

farming

Scientists

Across the world, scientists are working out how much water we all use. They can help world leaders decide how best to take action. Scientists also come up with clever inventions for cleaning and reusing water.

The movable WOTA Box is an invention that cleans wastewater.

The solar- and wind-powered SunSpring Hybrid purifies water.

environmentalist   campaigner   world leader

farmer

Farming

The world's biggest water user is farming. World leaders must work with farmers to understand what they can do to reduce the amount of water used while still producing enough food.

Campaigners

International campaigns help to raise awareness. They get people talking about important water issues such as cleaning pollution from our rivers.

Water connections

Many groups across the world are working together to show how we can protect our water. World leaders must unite in listening to these groups so that everyone in the future has a clean, reliable source of water.

what can I do
to save
water?

Water is needed to make all of the things we use every day. If you are lucky enough to live where it is available on tap, then the idea of it running out may be hard to imagine. But our planet does not have an endless supply of fresh, clean water, so we all need to play our part in protecting it.

save water

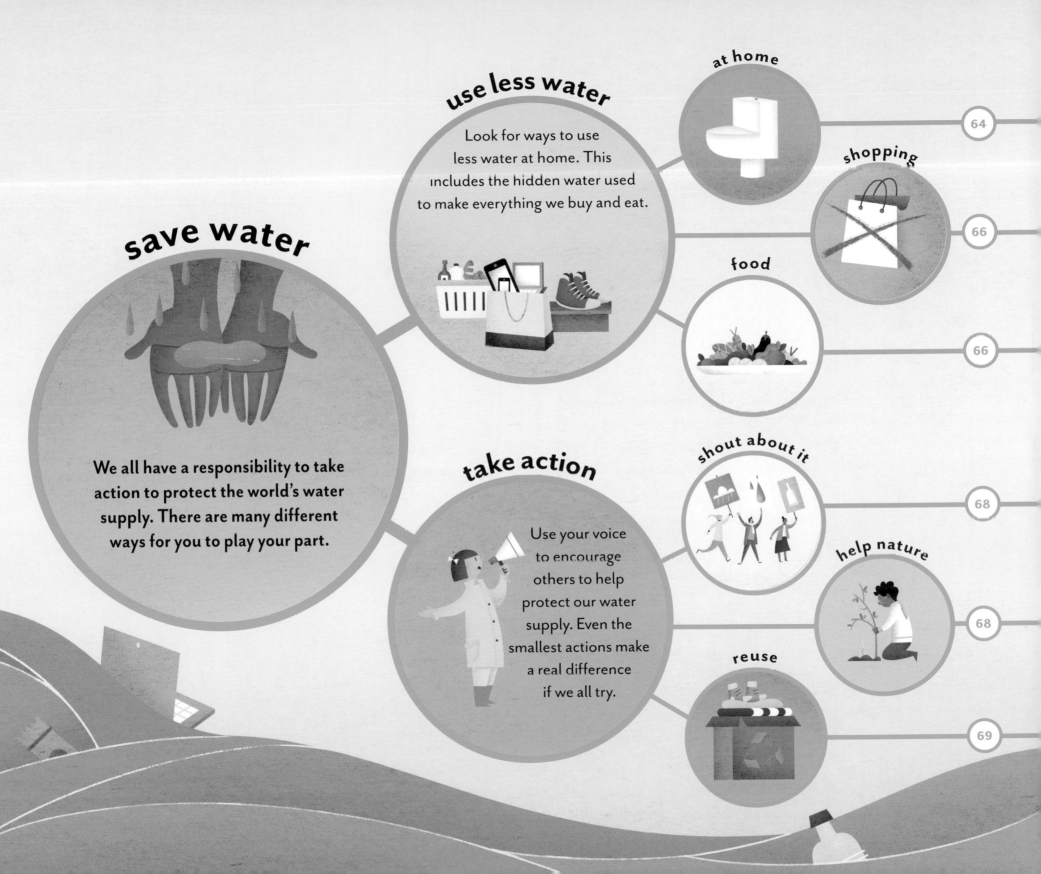

We all have a responsibility to take action to protect the world's water supply. There are many different ways for you to play your part.

use less water

Look for ways to use less water at home. This includes the hidden water used to make everything we buy and eat.

at home

64

shopping

66

food

66

take action

Use your voice to encourage others to help protect our water supply. Even the smallest actions make a real difference if we all try.

shout about it

68

help nature

68

reuse

69

Be water smart

Think about all the different ways you use water at home. Which small changes could you make to use less water? Some actions are easy–such as keeping clothes out of the laundry basket until they really need a wash. Other actions may take a little planning, or need you to break old habits and make new ones. There are many ideas to get you started.

watering plants

45

Free water!
Ask your family to set up a water barrel to collect the rainwater that runs off the roof of your home. It can be used instead of tap water for lots of useful things.

Home car wash
The rainwater collected by water barrels can be used for washing cars, bikes, and dirty boots.

Eco-friendly
Watering the plants with rainwater is better for them and the planet.

Better materials

Think before you clean up! All sorts of things washed down the drain can pollute the water supply. Switch to more eco-friendly materials and toiletries instead.

turning off taps

Avoid washing chemicals and tiny plastics such as glitter down the sink.

Brush smart

Leaving the tap running when you brush your teeth or wash your hands wastes gallons of water every day. Get in the habit of turning off the tap when you do not need water.

Toilet block

Almost a third of the water used in homes is flushed down the toilet. An easy way to save water each time you flush is to ask your parents to fit a brick in the tank.

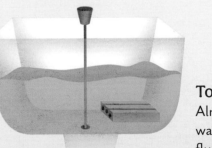

Drink smart

Running the cold tap to get a cooler drink wastes water. Why not keep a jug of water in the fridge instead. It is also said to make the water taste even better!

Water connections

Being smart with how you use water at home can make a difference. Even small savings can add up to a lot of water if we all try. See if you can get your family and friends to change their habits too.

59

changing habits

Use less of everything

We use water in nearly every area of our lives—for drinking, cooking, and washing. But much bigger amounts of water are used in farming and industry. It is vital for growing or making everything we need on a daily basis, from the cotton in the shirt on your back to drilling oil out of the ground to create your plastic toothbrush. So another great way to reduce your water footprint and protect Earth's water supply is to buy less stuff!

Eat less meat
Almost a tenth of all the fresh water used by people each year is for farming animals. Beef is by far the most water-hungry food to produce. It takes more than 600 gallons of water to make enough beef for just a single burger.

Buy fewer clothes
Cotton is one of the thirstiest crops because it grows best in warm climates. It takes 18 bathtubs full of water to grow enough cotton to make a single T-shirt!

Eat less sugar
Sugar cane is a crop greedy for water, and the more sugar we eat, the more sugar cane is planted. We do not need sugar in our diets, so saying no more often to sweet treats is a healthy way to reduce your water footprint.

Making shoes and trainers—particularly leather ones—uses huge amounts of water.

Wash clothes less often
Washing clothes uses lots of water. Washing human-made fabrics also releases tiny plastic fibers into the water. Wear clothes for longer before you wash them.

Water everywhere

Every time we turn on the tap, we waste at least some water. But our water use is far more than just what we see going down the drain. Everything we buy and eat takes a huge amount of water to produce.

Water connections

Nearly everything you buy or have at home has used several gallons of water before it even reaches you. Buying fewer things and eating less meat will make a big difference to the amount of water that is available for everyone.

Turn off your device

Generating electricity uses lots of water to make steam to power turbines. Always switch off your devices when they are fully charged!

Far from the taps

Just one in every ten gallons of fresh water reaches the taps. The rest is hidden water that may be used thousands of miles away to make plastic, food, or toys. Buying less will reduce your water footprint.

It takes at least twice as much water to make a plastic water bottle as the amount of water contained in the bottle!

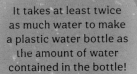

water use

Don't waste paper

More than 450 million tons of paper is produced every year. Wood may be renewable, but making paper has a big water footprint. Try to reduce what you use.

Spread the word

You may be too young to make the rules in your country, your school, or even your house, but you are never too young to influence other people. By coming up with ideas about how you can make changes in your own life, you can inspire others to take action, too. You can start a chain reaction that teaches other people about their water use and improves life for them and the planet.

leading the way

60

Use your voice

Shout about the water issues that matter to you. Talk to your friends and family about water to get them to help, too. Research young activists such as Autumn Peltier and Mari Copeny to find out how they make their voices heard.

Look after nature

Trees and plants suck up and filter water. They also keep groundwater levels topped up by stopping water trickling away in streams. Planting more trees and protecting local wildlife is a great way to help look after the water supply in your area.

Find out more

Read about water in books or online, or ask your teacher if your class can learn more about it in school. You could suggest going on a school trip to a dam, reservoir, or water treatment plant with an education program to find out how they work.

clothes

Water connections

We must all do whatever we can to reduce our water use and protect the world's water supply. By showing others the way, your actions can make a difference in many people's lives.

Monitor water use

It is better to take showers than baths because they use less water. You could compare how long you, your family, and friends spend in the shower to monitor how much water you all use.

Little steps

Trying to tackle everything at once would be overwhelming. Start with just one way people at home or school could use less water. This could be by eating more vegetables instead of meat. Come up with a plan to help them change.

Encourage reuse

New clothes are made using lots of water, so find fun ways to get others involved in reusing what they have instead. You could organize a clothes-swapping party, and encourage people to swap clothes, toys, and games rather than buy new things.

Glossary

algae Small plantlike living things that can make their own food using energy from sunlight.

aqueduct A human-made channel that carries water somewhere, usually a bridge across a valley.

aquifer A large underground water source.

atmosphere The layer of gases that surrounds the Earth.

atom Tiny particles that are the building blocks of everything.

biofuel A fuel made from the waste of living things, such as crops or food waste.

cell The smallest working part of a living thing. Billions of cells work together to help living things function.

cell membrane A very thin layer that surrounds the contents of a cell.

climate The typical pattern of weather over a long period of time.

climate change The ongoing changes to the world's climate.

cloud seeding Adding a substance to clouds to make raindrops form.

condense The change from a gas into a liquid, caused by cooling.

contaminated Being polluted with something that should not be there.

cytoplasm The jellylike liquid that fills the insides of cells.

dam A barrier built to stop or change the flow of water. Dams can be human-made or animal-made.

dehydration When a person's body does not have the amount of water it needs to work properly.

desalination When salt is removed from seawater to turn it into fresh water.

drought A shortage of water, usually caused when less rain falls on an area than normal.

ecosystem A community of living things that depend on each other and their environment in many ways.

evaporate The change from a liquid into a gas, caused by heating.

fertilizer A chemical that helps plants to grow faster and bigger.

filter The process of removing unwanted particles or pollutants from a liquid.

flooding When land that is normally dry becomes covered with water.

fossil fuel An energy-containing fuel, such as coal, oil, or natural gas, formed from the remains of plants or animals that lived millions of years ago.

glacier A huge, slow-moving river of ice.

gravity A force of attraction between different objects. It makes things fall to the ground on Earth.

groundwater Water that is found underground, often in the tiny spaces between soil particles or rocks.

habitat The place where an animal or plant usually lives or grows.

irrigation The supply of water to crops or other plants to help them grow.

microbe A tiny living thing that can only be seen under a microscope, such as a single bacterium.

migration The movement of people to a new area or country.

molecule A group of atoms bonded together. A molecule of water is made from two hydrogen atoms bonded to one oxygen atom. Everything is made of molecules.

pollution When a substance with harmful effects is found in or added to an environment.

precipitation Water that falls from the atmosphere as rain, snow, sleet, or hail.

recycling When used or waste material is turned into something that can be used again.

reservoir A large natural or human-made body of water used as a source of water.

sap A liquid that moves around inside plants, carrying water, food, and other substances to different parts of the plant.

sewage The water and waste material from homes and buildings that flows into underground channels called sewers.

smart technology Modern machinery and methods that collect data and use artificial intelligence to carry out tasks.

states The forms water is found in at normal temperatures on Earth—solid, liquid, and gas.

surface water Water that has collected on the surface of the ground—in rivers, lakes, wetlands, and oceans.

wastewater Water that has been used in homes, businesses, or industry.

water cycle The continuous journey that water makes from the sea to the sky, onto the land, and back to the sea.

water footprint The amount of fresh water being used in a particular place, by a certain process, or by a person or group of people.

water scarcity When there is not enough fresh water in an area to meet demand.

water stress When more than a quarter of the fresh water in an area is being used by people.

water table The level below the surface where water can be found.

water treatment The cleaning of wastewater to remove dirt and germs.

water vapor Water in the form of a gas.

watershed An area of land from which water drains into a river system or lake.

well A hole sunk into the ground to reach and bring up water.

Index

AB
aquifers 36–37, 48, 56
bacteria 12, 38, 41

C
campaigning 61, 63, 68–69
cars 30–31, 64
cells 14, 18–19, 22
  animals 18, 19
  plants 18
  pressure 19
cleaning 24, 27, 28, 33, 38, 41, 58, 61
climate change 48, 50–51, 52
clothes 24, 25, 29, 30, 31, 45, 64, 66, 67, 69
condensation 10–11, 20, 21
coral reefs 47

D
dams 34, 39, 53
dehydration 22
desalination 39, 57
deserts 20–21
diseases 46
dissolving 12–13, 18, 19, 26
drains 40–41
drinking water 13, 22–23, 24, 25, 28, 39, 44, 45, 46
droughts 49, 50–51, 52, 57

E
Earth 6, 7, 8–13, 16–17, 44, 51, 66
  atmosphere 9, 10, 50
  color from space 6, 12
  life on 6, 7, 16–17
ecosystems 47, 55
energy 25, 30–31, 39, 57
  biofuels 31
  cooling 27, 28, 29
  electricity 24, 25, 30, 67
  fossil fuels 50
  heating 25, 26, 28, 29

living things 18–19, 22–23
  power stations 31, 47
environment 38, 41, 60
evaporation 10–11, 12, 17, 21, 23, 37

FGH
farming 25, 26–27, 48, 49, 51, 53, 57, 59, 60, 61, 66
  crops 26–27, 48
  drought resistance 57
  fertilizers 46
  irrigation 26, 51, 56, 57, 60
  livestock 26–27, 48, 49,
floods 50, 59
food 16, 18–19, 20, 23, 24, 25, 27, 29, 40, 48, 49, 51, 59, 61, 66, 67
  cooking 25, 28, 66
gardening 28, 45, 64
gravity 11, 18, 35
groundwater 34, 36, 50–51, 68
habitats 46, 48, 59

IL
ice 6, 8, 9, 11, 13, 16, 17, 57
  glaciers 8, 13, 34, 50
  ice caps 6, 8, 13, 16
  ice caps on Mars 17
  icebergs 8, 57
  water ice on Mercury 17
internet 24, 25, 30
leaks 39, 48, 58
living things 6, 7, 9, 14–23, 46, 47
  animals 14, 15, 16, 18–19, 20–21, 46–47
  humans 15, 16, 22–23, 46–47
  plants 14, 15, 16, 18–19, 20–21, 45, 46–47
  temperature 19, 20–21, 23

MN
manufacturing 24, 25, 30–31, 60
molecules, water 8, 18
mountains 8
new technology 56–57

OP
oceans and seas 8, 10, 11, 12, 16, 17, 40, 41, 47, 57
  ocean on Venus 17
  rising sea levels 50
  salt 12–13, 39, 57
  tides 8
paper 24, 31, 67
pollution 13, 26, 27, 40–41, 43, 46–47, 50, 58, 61
  chemicals 46, 47
  fatbergs 40
  food 40
  microbes 46
  oil spills 47
  pesticides 26
  plastic waste 40, 46–47

RS
recycling 7, 10, 11, 40, 41
reservoirs 32, 33, 34, 39, 45, 51, 68
sewage 40–41, 46
sources 13, 15, 21, 32–39, 45, 49, 51, 52–53, 56–57, 60
sport 23, 28
states of water 7, 8–9, 10, 50
Sun 10, 18
surface water 36–37, 50–51
  lakes 8, 11, 12, 13, 33, 34, 36, 37, 40, 41, 45, 46, 51
  rivers 8, 10, 11, 13, 16, 26, 33, 34–35, 36, 37, 39, 40, 41, 46–47, 53, 61
  streams 11, 32, 34, 68
swamps 8

TU
toilets 25, 28, 29, 40, 44, 45, 56, 58, 65, 66
toys 30, 69
transport 24, 30, 39, 44, 48–49
underground water 9, 13, 21
  rocks 8, 11, 12, 17, 34, 36
  soils 8, 12, 18, 21, 31, 34, 36, 37, 57

W
washing 28–29, 44, 45, 64–65, 66, 69
water cycle 7, 10–13, 40, 44, 48
water migration 52–53
water scarcity 42, 44–45, 48–49, 52, 56–57
water services 38–41
  wastewater 33, 40–41, 47, 58, 61
  water treatment 38–39, 40–41
water sources 12–13, 21, 33, 34–37, 38, 39, 49, 51, 52, 53, 54, 56–57
water stress 48–49, 51, 52, 56–57
water vapor 8, 10, 22
water wars 52–53
weather 50–51
  clouds 6, 10, 16, 57
  extreme 50–51
  fog and mist 8, 20, 21
  hail 8, 11
  rain 6, 11, 13, 20, 21, 26, 28, 30, 33, 34–35, 37, 39, 44–45, 46, 49, 50–51, 57, 64
  snow 8, 11, 13
  wind 10–11, 21, 50
wetlands 51, 60

Author: Isabel Thomas
Illustrator: El Primo Ramón
Consultant: Professor Sara Hughes, University of Michigan

Editor: George Maudsley
Designer: Tory Gordon-Harris

Copyright © EarthAware Kids, 2022

Published by EarthAware Kids
Created by Weldon Owen Children's Books
A subsidiary of Insight International, L.P.
PO Box 3088
San Rafael, CA 94912
www.insighteditions.com

Weldon Owen Children's Books:
Art Director: Stuart Smith
Senior Production Manager: Greg Steffen
Publisher: Sue Grabham

Insight Editions:
Publisher: Raoul Goff

ISBN: 978-1-64722-586-5
Manufactured, printed and assembled in China
First printing 2022 DRM0822